AF279172

Some Poems of
ROGER CASEMENT

SOME POEMS OF ROGER CASEMENT
Published in 2025 by
New Island Books
Glenshesk House
10 Richview Office Park
Clonskeagh
Dublin D14 V8C4
Republic of Ireland
www.newisland.ie

First published in 1918 by Talbot Press, Dublin
Introduction copyright © Seán Hewitt, 2025

The right of Roger Casement to be identified as the author of this work has been asserted in accordance with the provisions of the Copyright and Related Rights Act, 2000.

Print ISBN: 978-1-83594-013-6
eBook ISBN: 978-1-83594-014-3

British Library Cataloguing in Publication Data. A CIP catalogue record for this book is available from the British Library.

Product safety queries can be addressed to New Island Books at the above postal address or at info@newisland.ie.

Typeset by JVR Creative India
Cover design by Niall McCormack, hitone.ie
Printed by L&C Printing Group, Poland, lcprinting.eu

The paper used in this book comes from the wood pulp of sustainably managed forests.

New Island Books is a member of Publishing Ireland.

10 9 8 7 6 5 4 3 2 1

Some Poems of
ROGER CASEMENT

With a new introduction by Seán Hewitt

NEW ISLAND

CONTENTS

THE LIFE AND AFTERLIFE OF ROGER CASEMENT

1864 Born 1 September in Sandycove, County Dublin, the youngest child of four, to parents Anne Casement (née Jephson) and Captain Roger Casement. The family is Church of Ireland but Anne secretl)y baptises the children in the Catholic Church. The family is chronically in debt and moves many times.

1873 Anne Casement dies and the family moves to County Antrim. Roger attends Ballymena diocesan school.

1877 Roger's father dies and he and his siblings are cared for by relatives in County Antrim and Liverpool. As a teenager, Roger becomes interested in Irish rebels of the past.

1879 At fifteen, Roger begins work as a clerk in the Elder Dempster shipping company, Liverpool.

1883 Casement becomes a purser (administration and logistics) on a ship bound for West Africa.

1884–

1891 Lives in the Congo Free State, founded and owned by King Leopold II of Belgium from 1885 to 1908.

1890 Meets Joseph Conrad, novelist and story writer.

1892 Works as a surveyor and customs official in the Niger Coast protectorate. Joins the British consular service. From 1895 onwards, holds consular appointments in various locations in Africa, including Luanda, Lourenço Marques (later Maputo) and Boma in the Congo.

1899 Joseph Conrad's *Heart of Darkness* is published.

1903 Is commissioned to investigate reports of atrocities carried out by King Leopold's agents in the Congo; gathers much evidence of forced labour, extortionate taxes, mutilation, murder and depopulation.

1904 Casement's report is published in February.

1904–

1906 Because of ill health, Casement takes a break from his consular career and spends 18 months in Ireland and Britain; he has no base and stays in lodgings, hotels and with friends. Becomes a committed Irish nationalist, supporting the ideals of 'Irish Ireland', the revival of the Irish language and rejecting empire in all its manifestations.

1905 Awarded the companion of the Order of St Michael and St George (CMG) in Edward VII's birthday honours list for his reporting on the Congo; Casement never opens the parcel containing the insignia of his award.

1906 Despite reluctance by the Foreign Office to reemploying him, Casement resumes his consular career and takes up postings in Brazil, culminating in his appointment as consul-general in Rio de Janeiro.

1908 As a result of several pressures, including Casement's 1904 report, the Belgian government takes over administration of the Congo. Casement is directed to investigate reports of atrocities in the rubber industry in the region of the Putumayo, Peru.

1911 Casement receives a knighthood from the British Empire but is embarrassed by this. Commits further to Irish causes and advocates for a fully independent Ireland; is galvanised by the opposition of Ulster Unionists to Home Rule.

1912 Casement's final report on the Putumayo is published to widespread publicity and praise; he gains an international reputation as a humanitarian.

1913 Retires from the Foreign Office. At the age of forty-nine, he begins to play a greater role in Irish affairs, becoming a member of the provisional committee of the Irish Volunteers.

1914 Leads the Howth gun-running in July, importing 1,500 rifles and ammunition from Belgium (some of these weapons would be used two years later during the Easter Rising). By August, when the guns land in Ireland, he is already in the United States raising funds for the Volunteers; he becomes a hero among Irish Americans but the outbreak of the First World War diverts attention away from Ireland's cause. Travels to Berlin in October where he tries to persuade the German government to declare support for Ireland; he receives reports that the British authorities are disconcerted by his actions and are offering substantial sums of money for information leading to his capture.

1914–

1916 Spends eighteen months in Germany trying but failing to induce Irish prisoners of war to change sides and to join an 'Irish brigade' to liberate Ireland (or Egypt); overall he fails in his mission in Germany. Casement's health deteriorates. Hears that an insurrection is planned for Easter 1916. Knowing Germany's support for this will be insufficient and fearing significant loss of life, he travels to Ireland to try to stop it.

1916 Casement is arrested at Banna Strand in County Kerry in April, before the Rising begins. The Aud, transporting German rifles, is intercepted by the British navy and is scuttled by her captain. Casement is brought to the Tower of London and tried for high treason in the Old Bailey in June; neither side mentions Casement's efforts to prevent the rising. Casement's trial lasts just four days and it takes the jury less than an hour to find him guilty on 29 June; he makes an eloquent speech from the dock; his knighthood is cancelled. Support for Casement grows in the UK and the US; in response, British officials circulate pages from the so-called Black Diaries, purportedly written by Casement in 1903, 1910 and 1911 which make explicit reference to his sexual relations with men. After an appeal is rejected on 24 July, Roger Casement is hanged at Pentonville Prison on 3 August. He is fifty-one years old. His body is buried in the prison's yard.

1918 *Some Poems of Roger Casement* is posthumously published by Talbot Press, Dublin, and includes an introduction by his cousin, Gertrude Parry.

1953 Casement Park, Belfast, home of Antrim GAA, is opened.

1965 Casement's remains are transferred from Pentonville and reburied in Glasnevin Cemetery in March, a symbolic gesture of goodwill between the Irish and UK governments. President Éamon de Valera speaks during the state funeral. Soon after, sculptor Oisín Kelly is commissioned by the Irish government for a statue commemorating Casement's life intended for his new grave.

1966 Fifty years after the Easter Rising, Tralee South train station is renamed Tralee Casement, as Córas Iompair Éireann (later Irish Rail) renames 15 major stations around the country in honour of the executed Republican leaders.

1971 Oisín Kelly completes his statue but because of the political environment, i.e., the Troubles, and the complex debates still raging over Casement's identity and his sexuality, the diaries and his mixed legacy, the statue enters storage for years.

1984 Kelly's statue is finally erected in Ballyheigue, County Kerry, overlooking Banna Strand, and is unveiled in September. Earlier in the same week, a cargo of armaments – destined for the IRA – had been intercepted off the Kerry coast. As a result, tensions are high in the area during the ceremony.

2002 Jeffrey Dudgeon, biographer and gay rights activist, publishes *Roger Casement: The Black Diaries, With a Study of His Background, Sexuality and Irish Political Life* arguing for the authenticity of the diaries.

2003 Angus Mitchell, historian and cultural critic, publishes *Casement* which makes the case for the diaries being forgeries.

2015 Ireland becomes the first country in the world to vote in favour of same-sex marriage.

2016 Centenary commemorations of the Easter Rising include many special mentions of Casement. *GCN*'s cover story in April is 'Casement and the Queering of 1916'. Brexit sees the United Kingdom vote to leave the European Union. In this context, Casement enters the public consciousness as a potentially uniting symbol of a united Ireland as well as an Irish queer icon.

2021   In September, Mark Richards' statue of Roger Casement is installed as part of the redeveloped Dun Laoghaire Baths in County Dublin.

Sources: *Dictionary of Irish Biography*, National Library of Ireland, the *Guardian*, *Breac*, *History Ireland* magazine, *GCN*, *New York Review of Books*

INTRODUCTION

Seán Hewitt

In Roger Casement's diary for 1903, the pages begin on Valentine's Day. All the pages from 1 January to the 13 February have been torn out. Though that might sound romantic, it was not the result of sentiment, and it was not a printer's error. The pages were not torn out by Casement himself, but by people who wished to expose him, to ruin his reputation by way of outing him to journalists. Along with containing explicit details of his sexual escapades, those pages also contained the drafts of his poetry. In fact, the Irish gay activist and great Casement scholar Jeffrey Dudgeon, in his edition of *The Black Diaries*, confirms that, among those torn out pages was a sexually-charged poem – a poem which opens provocatively with the line 'A big mouth choked with love'.

This is not the only poem of Casement's that reads as evidence of his homosexuality. Another, 'The Nameless One', survives, though not in its original form. Harbouring echoes of Lord Alfred Douglas's famous definition of homosexuality as 'the love that dare not speak its name', this poem is a contested artefact. Some consider it a forgery, others suspect that Casement simply copied it out, and that it was authored by someone else. Either way, the fact that it exists, written in Casement's hand, is telling. It seems unlikely that the British would have gone so far as to forge poems, when Casement's diaries are as explicit as they are; and if Casement did merely copy it out, why was he so taken with it? Either question seems, to me, to point towards the poem as revealing evidence of Casement's self-conscious sense of his own sexuality, and also his desire to form that sense of distance and desire into verse:

Love took me by the heart at birth
And wrought out from its common earth –
With soul at his own skill aghast –
A furnace my own breath should blast.

Why this was done I cannot tell
The mystery is inscrutable.
I only know I pay the cost
With heart and soul and honour lost.

The poem, in a neat and memorable couplet, seems to summarise so much of the condition of the closeted man: 'I sought by love alone to go / Where God had writ an awful no.'

Though I do not think it is possible that Casement read the poems of another closeted Victorian, Gerard Manley Hopkins, the tenor of thought in 'The Nameless One' also echoes lines from Hopkins's sonnet 'To seem the stranger', which also seems rife with suppressed feeling, and was written in Dublin sometime around 1884–85:

I am in Ireland now; now I am at a thírd
Remove. Not but in all removes I can
Kind love both give and get. Only what
    word
Wisest my heart breeds dark heaven's
    baffling ban
Bars or hell's spell thwarts.

The difficulty with charting the lives of queer historical figures such as Casement and Hopkins is that a fundamental aspect of their lives was, out of necessity, suppressed, and acted on in secret, if at all. 'Dark heaven's baffling ban', or the place where 'God had writ an awful no', extends outwards from their own lives and into the writing of history, so that they are censored even in the grave. The love that dare not speak its name is silenced, and the evidence of it is carefully and deliberately eroded from history.

The archive of Casement's life is not only erased, but contested, and so suspicion is thrown everywhere. During the trial for his part in the 1916 Easter Rising, pages from a number of diaries, termed the 'Black Diaries', were distributed to influential members of the public and press, with the intention of smearing Casement's reputation. These diaries, from 1903, 1910 and 1911, contained detailed, explicit, and rapacious accounts of Casement's sex life. A number of Irish nationalists contended (and still contend) that these diaries were forged by the British in order to smear Casement's name. What, after all, could be more of a stain on the life of a national hero? And, implicit in the nationalist response, was the question: could an Irish hero also be a homosexual? For the best part of a century, the answer was surely not. As Eoin Ó Máille wrote in his pamphlet *The Vindication of Roger Casement* (1994), 'freedom by a pervert would be a perverted freedom, and not acceptable.'

Casement was hanged, but the controversies flared and persisted. Now, the case seems clearer:

Casement was both a homosexual and anti-colonial hero. The diaries are, of course, real. For queer people in Ireland, this is a knotty history. With so much evidence of historical queer desire wiped from existence, the fact of these diaries is a rare proof. But it remains that the only reason they are widely known is because they were distributed, against Casement's will. The legacy we have, then, is both a treasure, and one that is mired in prejudice on both the Irish nationalist and the British governmental sides of the argument. In a rare moment of consonant opinion, both sides could agree on one thing at least: that homosexuality was a slander, and one strong enough to buckle the reputation of a great man.

The history of Casement-as-Poet is a minor one. Often, if a poem is bad, it is because it cloaks itself in cliché, in a borrowed costume of images and affectations. In other words, it has little of its own personality, or the personality of its maker. It seems clear that these poems do not reflect the intense brightness of the man's mind and life. In *Poems of the Irish Revolutionary Brotherhood*, published in Boston in 1916 in the aftermath of the Easter Rising, Padraic Colum and Edward O'Brien gathered together a selection of poems by four poets: Thomas MacDonagh, Padraic Pearse, Joseph Mary Plunkett and Roger Casement. An introduction by Colum charts the lives of these poets, but focuses chiefly on the first three. 'The years that brought maturity to the three poets who were foremost to sign, and foremost to take arms to assert, Ireland's Declaration of Independence, may come to be looked back on as signal days in Irish history. They were days of preparation.'

Turning back over the years of the Irish Revival – the efforts to revive the language, sport, crafts and mythologies of the nation – Colum gives relatively lengthy biographical sketches of each man in turn. Of the introduction's twenty-seven pages, only about 150 words are given to Casement, and only two of his poems, 'In the Streets of Catania' and 'Hamilcar Barca', a sonnet, are included. This may have been part of a sentiment that has sometimes resurfaced in opinions on Casement, namely that he spent those 'days of preparation' not in a passion for Ireland, but in service to the British Foreign Office and, of course, in his humanitarian exposés of the atrocities of colonialism in the Congo and the Putumayo.

In an elliptical note, Colum half-excuses himself: Casement's 'life has been all action', he says, 'and the poems he has written so few'. And then, 'If poetry comes out of intensity of vision Roger Casement was potentially a great poet.' Colum's reticence is noticeable, not only in his grouping of Casement along with the other poets, but also in his reluctance to praise Casement's poems. Casement the man had 'intensity of vision', Casement the poet had only 'potential'.

Some Poems of Roger Casement was first published in 1918, two years after Roger Casement was executed in August 1916 for his role in the Easter Rising. Gertrude Parry, Casement's cousin, began her introduction to that volume in a vein not dissimilar to Padraic Colum. 'In giving these few poems of Roger Casement to the Irish people', she wrote, 'I do not claim for them any special value as Irish literature.' Over the years, Roger Casement's ghost has been the subject of endless controversies, co-opted into both the queer liberation movement in Ireland and the Republican movement. Predator or saviour, traitor or hero, maligned martyr or gay icon? The question depends on who you ask, and what aspects of Casement's life they choose to hold in focus, or to dismiss as a lie.

As Colm Tóibín notes in his brilliant essay, 'Roger Casement: Sex, Lies and the Black Diaries', John Bruton, the former Taoiseach, when he was reviewing Dudgeon's 2002 biography and new edition of the Black Diaries, did not see the relevance of Casement's private life to any understanding of his public actions. Bruton ignored the question of Casement's homosexuality until a final paragraph, where he made the strange comment that 'these diaries have no literary, and now little historical value, and should not have been given so much space in an otherwise stimulating, fair and well-written book.' The same comment could be made about Casement's verse. But if Bruton is wrong here, as he certainly is, then what claim could we make for Casement's poems?

His are not the restless lyrics of Eva Gore-Booth, or the visionary and weird poems of Æ, and they do not have the music and melancholy of Padraic Pearse. Of course, we do not expect our revolutionaries to have the literary genius of Yeats, or of Synge, or of Lady Gregory. Though much ink has been spilled on the idea that the Irish revolution was shaped by literature, and was in many ways a production of the stage and the imagery of blood sacrifice, nevertheless, for the most part, the writers wrote, and the revolutionaries took action.

The poems in this book are just a small portion of numerous poems written by Casement, some of which were more revealing and intimate, though they are either lost or their authorship is questioned. Still, if these poems seem slight, or of little literary value, they are nevertheless evidence of a need in Casement to respond in verse to political and personal events. Indeed, it may not be pushing the point too far to suggest that the evidence of the so-called Black Diaries attest to a similar function to narrate, record, and respond to the experience of living. There may also be room to speculate, within reason, about the potentially coded nature of these poems. For the most part, the poems in this book are love poems. 'The Heart's Verdict', 'Mio Salvatore', 'Love's Horizon', 'Love's Cares', all written between 1892–95, when Casement was in his late twenties, suggest his affinity for established romantic and possibly erotic tropes. 'Mio Salvatore', for example, may be a literal address to the saviour, Christ, but it seems more likely that it is a love poem cloaked in the guise of a religious poem:

> Were I a king, my crown of gold
> I should not for a moment hold,
> Did not thy brow its glory share,
> Were thou not even next my chair.

There is passion here, and a longing for human devotion. Or, in 'Love's Cares', is there some double-meaning in the fact that Casement chooses to personify Love using masculine rather than feminine pronouns, so that we get the potential homoeroticism of lines like 'He sleeps where never a comb has passed, / And holds his breath in the tiny snare / Of a curl his kiss shall undo at last'?

There is also, of course, the political Casement in these poems, one of which calls for the repatriation of the Elgin Marbles, and another (a translation from the French of Victor Hugo) begins:

I hate oppression with a hate profound,
And wheresoever in the wide world round,
Beneath a traitor king, a cruel sky,
I hear appeal a strangled people's cry –

It is clear that Casement sought a language and a form for both his sense of injustice and his passionate susceptibility to romance and desire. This collection offers an insight into Casement's work in poetry, and gives us tantalising glimmers of his emotional and intellectual life. We have, in these pages, some shadowed insight into the man, and though these poems may not satisfy our sense of him as impassioned, intelligent, erotic, they nevertheless exist as a gesture towards a broader archive, whether that archive be lost or contested.

Casement is a man whose writing has been used to both condemn and celebrate him, to throw him down to the level of a deviant, and to elevate him to an almost-saintlike martyrdom. He is also a man who has undergone metamorphoses in death – the ghost of Roger Casement, as Yeats had it, has been knocking at the door for over a century, calling to some in the cause of Irish Republicanism, to others for the cause of anti-imperialism, and to others for queer rights, and for many in for the cause of all three. In these poems, we have another aspect of him, and one in which we can hear his voice. In this book, we meet a Casement compelled by sound, language, romance and love, to speak back into the world, to set something of his heart and his mind to music.

'THE HEART'S VERDICT'

Oh! Hearts that meet, and hearts that part!
The world is full of sorrow:
Men love and die—th' almighty mart
Puts up new hearts to-morrow.

Was this Creation's scheme at start?
Oh! Then I little wonder
That Lucifer's proud human heart
Preferred to God His thunder.

'MIO SALVATORE'

'Were I a king, my crown of gold
I should not for a moment hold,
Did not thy brow its glory share,
Were thou not ever next my chair.

'Were I a God, my heaven would be
One long, lone, vast sterility,
Eternal only in its woe
Did thou not all its purpose know.

'Were I a saint, my midnight cell
Would be the portico of hell,
Did not my scourging heart attest
Thy love dwells in a stricken breast.'

'LOVE'S HORIZON'

Love is the salt sea's savour,
Love is the palm-tree's sheen,
Love is the sky of evening,
That softly sets between.

Love is the ocean's purple,
Love is the mountain's crest,
Love is the golden Eagle
That hither builds his nest.

The wind that lists at morning.
The first song of the bird,
The leaves that stir so lightly
Before a limb has stirred:

These are my love's harbingers

By gathering music drawn.

Oh! Wake my love and own them,

Thou life voice of the Dawn.

'LOVE'S CARES'

Oh! What cares Love for a sunburst skin?
Love laughs and sighs for it all the same;
Love seeks a blush that is far within
From the glow of his asking eyes that came—

Oh! What cares Love for untidy hair?
He sleeps where never a comb has passed,
And holds his breath in the tiny snare
Of a curl his kiss shall undo at last—

Oh! What cares Love for a tender heart?
His eyes are filled to their glorious brim;
On tears, on tears from a shining start
Love bears it gently away with him.

Oh! What cares Love for a wounded breast?

Love shows his own with a broader scar:

'Tis only those who have loved the best

Can say where the wounds of loving are.

THE PEAK OF THE CAMEROONS

I.

The Heavens rest upon thee that the eye

Of man may not, for when thou sittest hid

In thunderstorm of lofty pyramid

Of thwarting sea-cloud whitening up the sky,

Then are the clouds set on thee to forbid

*That man should share the mystery of Sinai;

Then are thy ashen cones again bestrid

By living fire—impenetrably nigh.

* To this line there is a note: – 'This line is admissible in a sonnet.'

For thus, by the Dualla, art thou seen,
Home of a God they know, yet would not know;
But I, who far above their doubts have been
Upon thy forehead hazardous, may grow
To fuller knowledge, rooted sure and slow
Where lava slid—like pines Enceladine.

II.

And I have seen thee in the West's red setting
Stand like some Monarch in a crimson field,
With fleeing clouds empurpling as they yield.
And sunset still the glorious sham abetting.
While high above thy purple forest's fretting
Thy mighty chest in tranquil gold concealed,
And on thy brows of the dead days begetting
A light that comes from higher things revealed.

So shows there in a passing soul's transgression

A light of hope beyond these prison bars

Divinely rendered, that, when doubting mars

Our day's decline, we still may find progression

Of light to light, as day with silent cession

Makes o'er to night—articulate with stars.

HAMILCAR BARCA

Thou that didst mark from Heircte's spacious hill
The Roman spears, like mist, uprise each morn,
Yet held, with Hesper's shining point of scorn,
Thy sword unsheathed above Panormus still;
Thou that were leagued with nought but thine own
    will,
Eurythmic vastness to that stronghold torn
From foes above, below, where, though forlorn,
Thou still hadst claws to cling, and beak to kill—
Eagle of Eryx!—When the Ægation shoal
Rolled westward all the hopes that Hanno wrecked
With mighty wing, unwearying, didst thou
Seek far beyond the wolf's grim protocol,
Within the Iberian sunset faintly specked
A rock where Punic faith should bide its vow.

VERSES

(Sent from the Congo Free State in response to
Mr. Harrison's appeal for the Restoration of the
Elgin Marbles to Greece.)

Give back the Elgin marbles; let them lie
Unsullied, pure beneath an Attic sky.
The smoky fingers of our northern clime
More ruin work than all the ancient time.
How oft the roar of the Piraen sea
Through column'd hall and dusky temple stealing
Hath struck these marble ears, that now must flee
The whirling hum of London, noonward reeling.

Ah! let them hear again the sounds that float

Around Athene's shrine on morning's breeze,—

The lowing ox, the bell of climbing goat

And drowsy drone of far Hymettus' bees.

Give back the marbles; let them vigil keep

Where art still lies, o'er Pheidias' tomb, asleep.

Lukunga Valley,
Cataract Region of the Lower Congo

LOST YOUTH

(Written on receiving a letter from a friend, T.H., who had

spent the best years of his life as a missionary in Central Africa,

in which he speaks of 'the glorious superfluity of strength and

spirits one remembers as a lad, but alas! only remembers.')

Weep not that you no longer feel the tide

High breasting sun and storm, that bore along

Your youth on currents of perpetual song:

For in these mid-stream waters, still and wide,

A sleepless purpose the great deep doth hide;

Here spring the mighty fountains pure and

    strong,

That bear sweet change of breath to city throng,

Who, had the sea no breeze, would soon have died.

So though the sun shines not in such a blue,

Nor have the stars the meaning youth deviced,

The heavens are nigher, and a light shines through

The brightness that nor sun nor stars sufficed;

And on this lonely waste we find it true

Lost youth and love, not lost, are hid with Christ.

THE STREETS OF CATANIA

(The streets of Catania are paved with blocks of the lava of Aetna.)

All that was beautiful and just,
All that was pure and sad
Went in one little, moving plot of dust
The world called bad.

Came like a highwayman, and went,
One who was bold and gay,
Left when his lightly loving mood was spent
Thy heart to pay.

By-word of little streets and men,
Narrower theirs the shame,
Tread thou the lava loving leaves, and then
Turn whence it came.

Aetna, all wonderful, whose heart

Glows as thine throbbing glows,

Almond and citron bloom quivering at start,

Ends in pure snows.

THE IRISH LANGUAGE

It is gone from the hill and the glen—

The strong speech of our sires;

It is sunk in the mire and the fen

Of our nameless desires:

We have bartered the speech of the Gael

For a tongue that would pay,

And we stand with the lips of us pale

And all bloodless to-day;

We have bartered the birthright of men

That our sons should be liars.

It is gone from the hill and the glen,

The strong speech of our sires.

Like the flicker of gold on the whin

That the Spring breath unites,

It is deep in our hearts, and shall win

Into flame where it smites:

It is there with the blood in our veins,

With the stream in the glen,

With the hill and the heath and the weans

They shall *think* it again;

It shall surge to their lips and shall win

The high road to our rights—

Like the flicker of gold on the whin

That the sun-burst unites.

PARNELL

(October 6th, 1891.)

Hush—let no whisper of the cruel strife,

Wherein he fell so bravely fighting, fall

Nigh these dead ears; fain would our hearts recall

Nought but proud memories of a noble life—

Of unmatched skill to lead by pathways rife

With danger and dark doubt, where slander's

    knife

Gleamed ever bare to wound, yet over all

He pressed triumphant on—lo, thus to fall.

Through and beyond the breach he living made

Shall Erin pass to freedom and to will,

And shape her fate: there where his limbs are laid

No harsh reproach dare penetrate the shade;

Death's angel guards the door, and o'er the sill

A mightier voice than Death's speaks 'Peace, be

   still!'

BENBURB

Since treason triumphed when O'Neill was forced
    to foreign flight,
The ancient people felt the heel of Scotch
    usurper's might;
The barren hills of Ulster held a race proscribed
    and banned
Who from their lofty refuge viewed their own so
    fertile land.
Their churches in the sunny vales; the homes that
    once were theirs,
Torn from them and their Faith to feed some
    canting minion's prayers:
Oh Lord! from many a cloudy hill then streamed
    our prayers to Thee,

And like the dawn on summer hills, that only
    watchers see,
Thy glorious hope shone on us long before the
    sleeping foe
Knew that their doom had broken on the sword of
    Owen Roe.

'Twas dawn of fair June morning, while
    Blackwater still drew grey,
His valley'd mists about him that we saw at
    Killylea,
The Scottish colours waving as they headed to the
    ford
Where never foemen waded yet, but paid it with
    the sword;

And fair it was to see them in the golden morning
    light,
Climb up the hill by Caledon and turn them to the
    right;
As they neared Yellow Ford, where Bagnall met
    O'Neill,
Joy gathered in our throats and broke above their
    cannons' peal,
And oh! a thrill went through our ranks,
    as straining towards the foe,
Like hounds in leash we panted for the word of
    Owen Roe.

Not yet—altho' O'Ferrall's horse come riding in
    amain;
Not yet—altho' fierce Cunningham pursues with
    slackened rein;
Not yet—altho' in skirmish and in many a
    scattered fight
We hold them—still with waiting eye, O'Neill
    smiles in despite;
Till slanting on our backs the sun full on their
    faces fell.
Then blinding axe and battle spear rose with a
    sudden swell
'For God, and Church, and Country now—upon
    them every man;
But hold your strength until ye
    see them scarce a pike-length's span;

The Red Hand, ever uppermost, strike home your
    strongest blow';
And with a yell our feet outsped the words of
    Owen Roe.

Like heaving lift of yellow wave that drags the
    sandy shore
On with it to its foaming fall, our rushing pikemen
    bore
Horse, foot, and gun, and falling flags, like
    streamers of red wrack,
Torn from their dripping hold, in one broad swell
    of carnage back;
Stout Blayney's gallant horse withstood that
    seething tide in vain;

It bore them down, and redder raced with life-
     blood of the slain;
One regiment only fought its way from out that
     ghastly fight,
And Conway slew two horses on the Newry road
     that night;
While Monroe fled so fast he left both hat and wig
     to show
How full the breeze that lifted up the flag of Owen
     Roe.

Ho! Ironsides of Cromwell, ye've got grimmer
     work to do,
Than when on Naseby's ruddy morn your ready
     swords ye drew—

Than when your headlong charges routed Rupert's
    tried and best,
Ere yet the glare of battle fainted in the loyal West.
Those swords must break a stouter foe ere ye
    break Erin's weal
Or stamp your bloody title-deeds with
    Cromwell's bloodier seal;
The dead men of Elizabeth's red reign for
    comrades call,
The Scots we sent to-day have need of ye to bear
    their pall;
There's room for undertakers still, and none will
    say ye no
To such fair holdings—measured by the sword of
    Owen Roe.

Ho! ring your bells, Kilkenny town; ho! Dublin
    burghers pass
In open day, with open brow, to celebrate the
    Mass.
The Sword of State that Tudor hate laid sore on
    Church of God,
Hath fallen here with shattered hilt and vain point
    in the sod.
Ho! holy Rinnuncini, and ye high lords of the Pale
Lay by your sheets of parchment, and put on your
    sheeted mail,
For God hath spoke in battle, and His face the foe
    is toward,
And ye must hold by valour what He hath freed by
    sword.

Yea, God in fight hath spoken, and thro’ cloud
    hath bent His brow
In wrath upon the routed—but in hope o’er Owen
    Roe.

OLIVER CROMWELL

1650–1659

(Addressed to the Liberal Members who 'went back' on their previous vote and rejected the grant for his statue.)

'Tear out the page his hand hath writ in blood.'
Aye! tho' a decade filled with mighty deeds
That page records; what though in it the seeds
Of greater freedom sprung, than ever stood
On any shore, to shadow freedom's brood.
The lordly oak from which a fleet proceeds
May fall unhonoured; can mere party needs
Fill *your* hands too, with this consenting mud?
We Irishmen found only shade to die
Within the shadow of that mighty tree;
But you base Englishmen it bore on high,

And girt your commerce safe on many a sea:

O! may the people Cromwell taught, deny

Your right within these walls, and turn the key!

THE TRIUMPH OF HUGH O'NEILL

Beal an Altra Buidhe (The Fight of the Yellow Ford, 1598.)

Speed the joyful news of victory from Dungannon
    to Gweedore,
Let the shout of triumph echo 'mid the cliffs of
    dark Benmore,
Let the flame that gleams on Sperrin light a flame
    on every strand,
Till one mighty blaze shall tell it to all men
    throughout the land.

The haughty Saxon boasted he would ravage
    broad Tyrone,
And lay our fields in ashes, and make our flocks
    his own,

Nor hold his hand 'till humbled each Irish kerne
    should kneel
To England's monarch only, and not to Hugh O'Neill.

But vain was all his boasting, and vain was all he
    swore,
For, like the storms of winter when from the hills
    they pour,
With clouds of long-haired spearmen, and ranks
    of flashing steel,
O'er the broken host of Saxons swept the children
    of O'Neill.

Arquebus and gun were fired, yet were fired all in
    vain,
For their owners' heads were cloven by the
    lightening sweeping *skean*,
But the sturdy English yeomen, who had ne'er
    been known to reel,
Like the withered leaves of autumn, fell before the
    fierce O'Neill.

Blackwater's tide ran darker than e'er it ran before,
The 'Yellow Ford' was crimsoned, the fields were
    drenched with gore.
The Saxon host had vanished; and Armagh rang
    out a peal
Of triumph o'er the vanquished, and of welcome
    to O'Neill.

No more the feet of foemen shall taint our
    Northern soil,
No more the waving cornfields shall be the
    Saxon's spoil.
Our flag no longer drooping, each fold shall now
    reveal,
And wave for God and Erin and our darling Hugh
    O'Neill.

TRANSLATION FROM VICTOR HUGO'S 'FEUILLES D'AUTOMNE'

'I hate oppression with a hate profound,

And wheresoever in the wide world round,

Beneath a traitor king, a cruel sky,

I hear appeal a strangled people's cry—

Where mother Greece, by Christian kings

    betrayed

To butcher Turks, hangs disembowelled, flayed.

Where Ireland, bleeding on her Cross expires,

And German truth in vain fronts royal liars.

'Oh then, upon their heads my curse I launch,
These kings whose steeds pace bloody to the
    paunch:
I feel the poet speaks their judgment, and
The indignant Muse, with unrelenting hand,
Shall bind them pilloried to their thrones of
    shame,
And press their dastard crowns to shape a name
That on their brows the poet's hand shall trace—
So Man may read their calling in their face.'

ORIGINAL INTRODUCTION

Gertrude Parry (née Bannister), 1918

In giving these few poems of Roger Casement to the Irish people I do not claim for them any special value as Irish literature. Roger Casement was not a poet, he would have been the last to lay claim to any such title, but, like the greater part of his fellow-countrymen, he felt from time to time the impulse to express some particular thought in verse, and he used to jot down, sometimes in a letter to a friend, sometimes on an odd half sheet of paper, the thought clothed in a poetic form just as it came into his mind.

His was a nature of peculiar delicacy and refinement and of singular simplicity; he had but one passion, Ireland, but one deep sympathy—compassion for the helpless and oppressed.

Even as a little boy he turned with horror and revulsion from cruelty of every description: he would tenderly nurse a wounded bird to life, and stop to pity an overloaded horse. This gentleness and tender-heartedness was one of his most marked characteristics; it led him to champion the cause of the Congo native and the Putumayo Indian, and to spend his slender means in later life in trying to relieve the wretched fever-stricken inhabitants in Connemara when typhus was raging among them, or to provide a mid-day meal for children in the Gaeltacht, who after walking perhaps for miles to school, through storm and rain, would have gone hungry all day if his kindly heart had not pitied them. When he was stricken with misfortune, it was these same children whose touching letters to him and whose words of consolation, with their prayers, brought tears to his eyes.

The act which brought him to his death was the result of long years of brooding over Ireland and her destiny; it was not a sudden and new impulse as some have endeavoured to prove. To say that his interest in Ireland began with his retirement from the service of the British Foreign Office is to misrepresent the facts entirely. Roger Casement from his earliest days was before everything else a lover of Ireland. In his schooldays he begged from the aunt, with whom he spent his holidays, for possession of an attic room which he turned into a little study, and the writer remembers the walls papered with cartoons cut out of the *Weekly Freeman*, showing the various Irish Nationalists who had suffered imprisonment at English hands for the sake of their belief in Ireland a Nation. Many years later, when he himself was a prisoner in an English gaol he wrote: 'I have felt this destiny on me since I was a little boy; it was inevitable; everything in my life has led up to it.' He seemed in a curious way to have a foreboding of his fate. Once, years before his retirement, he was joking with a friend about some wonderful plan that was conceived in a mood of playfulness, and the carrying out of which would have involved considerable danger. The friend pointed out that the disadvantage of it all lay in the fact that they might accidentally kill someone, and 'then,' she added, 'we'd be hanged.' Roger Casement was silent for a moment, his deep-set eyes fixed on an invisible goal, and then he said very quietly, 'I think I shall be hanged for Ireland.' A friend tells me that later he made a similar observation to a man who spoke of old rebellions and the fate of their leaders, 'I shall be hanged, too, for leading an attack on Dublin Castle.'

An incident is told of his life in South Africa, about the time of the Boer War. He was one day, with two companions on the verandah of a hotel, when a lady who had been observing them from a distance for some time approached them. She excused herself for addressing strangers and explained that she had felt compelled to do so as they had interested her profoundly. Explaining that she had the gift of second-sight, she asked permission to tell their fortunes, to which they consented, looking upon the matter as a joke. Having told the fortunes of the lady and of the second companion, she turned at last to Roger Casement, and stated that his was the most interesting fate. She described his adventurous life in broad outline, and then said, 'You must take care: at the age of 52 you will come to a violent end.' Roger Casement was within a month of his fifty- second birthday when he died.

There was a curious remoteness about him at times. He used to sit for long periods silent in a reverie, and would awaken from it with a sudden start. In his habits he was always simple and frugal; he rose very early in the morning and was always at work before breakfast; he cared nothing for society in the worldly sense, but he loved his friends and was always and invariably happy in the company of children of all ages and classes. Once the writer was walking with him through the streets of an old country town when a tired woman after a shopping expedition was vainly urging an equally tired, and, I am bound to say, naughty little boy to 'come on.' When at last in exasperation she called out, 'Very well, I'll go home without you,' the culprit set up an ear-piercing yell and flung himself down on the ground. Roger turned round at once, to hasten back. 'Ah! poor soul,' he said, 'his heart is broken, God help him; I'll pick him up.'

Small children always adored him. The tiny three-year-old child of a charwoman working in the house where he was staying used to creep in from the kitchen, and try to catch his eye as he sat writing. He always had a smile and caress for her, and one day her mother found her trying with both hands to turn the handle of the study door and scolded her. She hung her head and said, 'I wanted to see the gentleman with the kind eyes.'

Many a little beggar child in Dublin knew the smile in those kind eyes, and they used to greet him with smiles in return and always get their copper or two. We used to tease him, and say he walked through the streets of Dublin 'buying smiles at a penny each.' I do not think any Irish man, woman, or child ever appealed to him for sympathy and help that he did not give.

On a motor tour through Donegal with some friends he met an old woman whose son and his wife had died and left to her care a family of small children. They looked poor and hungry, and the old woman found it hard to make her little farm support them all. 'Wouldn't they be better for some milk?' asked Roger, seeing them make a scanty meal, with water to drink. 'Indeed they would if I could be getting it for them,' said the grandmother. Roger made no answer, but at the next market town he bought a cow and had it sent out to the old lady.

It was in Ireland he always felt at home; he hated big cities, noise, music-halls, and restaurants. He wrote from London on one visit, 'I feel more and more of a foreigner here'; but in the Irish country, with the simple country folk, he was always content. One of the happiest experiences of his life in later years was a short visit he paid to Tory Island in 1912, when he organised a Ceilidh, to which everyone on the island was invited. He sat in the crowded schoolroom, watching the boys and girls dancing their reels and jigs, and listening to the Gaelic songs till far on into the night, when the Ceilidh broke up. He loved the Tory people and used to plan many times to go back and visit them. Tory has a sort of fascination about it, it looks so remote and unreal, 'like an opal jewel in a pale blue sea,' he described it once in a letter.

During all the time of his varied experiences abroad in Africa and South America, his mind turned always with longing and affection to Ireland. He looked upon himself as an Irishman before all things. He eagerly watched for the rare arrival of mails bringing word of Ireland and her doings. 'Send me news of Ireland,' he wrote from South America, 'and also what the papers say about the Congo, but chiefly Ireland; Ireland first, last, and for ever.'

Although not a rich man (he had no private means) he contributed generously to all Irish schemes for furthering the National life. He helped several of the Gaelic Colleges, gave prizes in schools for the study of Irish, and did his best to help along many of those newspapers and periodicals which were founded by young and hopeful Irishmen to expound their views and which alas! so often came to an untimely end.

With his singularly generous nature money mattered nothing at all to him save for the use he could make of it to help the work he had at heart. He spent little upon himself, in fact he denied himself all luxuries, and even comforts, that he might have to give to Irish causes or to the Irish poor. Those who said of him that he sold himself for money knew nothing of the man they were slandering. He was wholly indifferent to money for its own sake. His scrupulous integrity as to public funds was illustrated by the following:—When he was called to give evidence before a certain commission, as he was waiting his turn with others who had to travel to London for the same purpose, one of the secretaries remarked to a witness, 'Do you see that man?' (pointing to Roger Casement), 'Well, all the rest have charged first-class railway fares, but he has put down third.'

He wrote much on the Irish question. Letters from his pen appeared in many Irish newspapers, and not a few English ones, and his essays, which will, it is hoped, be published later, show not only a deep insight but much literary skill. His speech from the dock was described by a leading English literary man as an effort 'worthy of the finest examples of antiquity.'

At the age of 52 he came to a violent end … So have many others who died for Ireland; he stands among his peers, the Irish martyrs. He would not have chosen to die otherwise, the love of his life was Kathleen ni Houlihan; when he thought he heard her voice calling from her four green fields he had no choice but to obey, though he knew it led to death; but death which comes in such a form to the body leaves the spirit but freer to carry on its purpose.

The men of 1916 are not dead in any real sense, for

‘They shall be remembered for ever,
They shall be alive for ever,
They shall be speaking for ever,
The people shall hear them for ever.’